Print information available on the last page.

Rev. date: 04/27/2019

To order additional copies of this book, contact:
Xlibris
1-888-795-4274
www.Xlibris.com
Orders@Xlibris.com

LOST POET
From The Heart
God's Messenger

Frank V. Moran

TABLE OF CONTENTS

Nine Eleven *7*

In The Word of God's Bible *8*

Faith Is The Key *9*

The Extreme *10*

I Am *11*

Dark Cold Is The Night *12*

A Glimmer Of Hope *13*

So You thought You Killed This Race *14*

Young People *15*

Two Rocks *16*

You Can't Give A Life Back *17*

The Collective Works Of Frank V. Moran
Volume 1 – The Truth About Drugs *18*

DEDICATION

This book of rhythmic poetry is to enlighten all of God's children throughout the world, that their lives can be meaningful and fulfiling living drug free, and always keeping Jesus Christ at the head of their lives, God has given me vision and a new life in Christ Jesus. As drugs had over taken my life, I turned to God who delivered me out of the bondage of drugs. Thanks to my wife, Cathy A. Moran and my family, also my church family, and all God's children. For you are all my reason for living. That through God his son Christ Jesus and the Holy Spirit I can make a difference in this world. It doesn't matter the color of your skin. Don't be a slave to anyone or anything. With God's everlasting love, we who have been lifted out of darkness, whether it be drugs or any other sin must stand firm and lift up our brothers and sisters that they may feel the saving power of God through Jesus Christ.

1/19/2002
Frank V. Moran

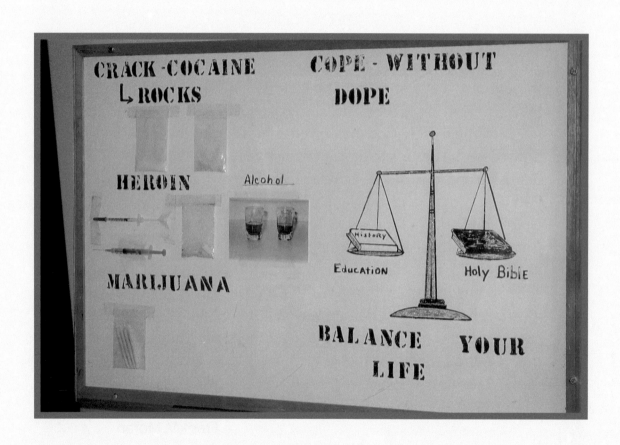

6

NINE ELEVEN

Nine eleven was a tragic day, most people asked why did it happen that way? Two twin towers standing tall and strong, in a matter of minutes they both were blown, up in smoke the buildings they fell. In my mind I heard the people yell, one plane after another as my brothers and sisters were killed, was it truly the Bible being fulfilled. The mayor of the city, yes, the man of the hour must have been running off God given power.

And what of our president? Who took to the sky, but handled the situation as time went by, rallied the people and and that's no lie.

Their were two other planes that went down that day, they gave of their lives in a special way, they were more than heroes. Without a doubt, the love they showed makes me want to shout. Bin Laden you had no remorse you entered this country like the trojan horse, you killed our firemen, and our policemen, and many others none of the lest, were going to drive you back into the Middle East, because the God I serve says we will have peace. America the beautiful, oh so bold, many different races standing in one fox hole. Remember God is all power if you want to be blessed, and his son, Jesus will do the rest.

Frank V. Moran
1-19-2002

IN THE WORD OF GOD'S BIBLE

IN THE WORD OF GOD'S BIBLE, AND IT TELLS OF OUR TRIBAL.
YOU SEE GOD CREATED MAN, YET HE HAD A MASTER PLAN.
IN THE WORD IN THE WORD OF GOD'S BIBLE AND IT TELLS
OF OUR TROUBLE.
MY SON YOU MUST BE BRAVE, BECAUSE YOU WERE BORN A SLAVE.
IN THE WORD IN THE WORD OF GOD'S BIBLE, CHILDREN YOU
DON'T HAVE TO WORRY YOU WILL SOON SEE GOD'S GLORY
IN THE WORD OF GOD'S BIBLE AND IT TELLS OF OUR SORROW,
NOW YOU HAVE TO TAKE A STAND IF YOU CALL YOURSELF A MAN,
IN THE WORD IN THE WORD OF GOD'S BIBLE, IF YOU WANT TO
FIGHT THE FIGHT YOU HAVE TO CALL ON JESUS CHRIST,
IN THE WORD OF GOD'S BIBLE, I DON'T KNOW WHICH ONE I LOVE
THE MOST FATHER, SON OR HOLY GHOST,
IN THE WORD OF GOD'S BIBLE.
THIS STORY IS NOT A MYSTERY, IT IS ALL PART OF HISTORY IN THE
WORD, IN THE WORD OF GOD'S BIBLE IF YOU WANT TO SEE THE
PROMISED LAND
FIRST PUT YOUR HAND IN GOD'S HAND,
IN THE WORD IN THE WORD OF GOD'S BIBLE

Frank V. Moran
1-19-2002

FAITH IS THE KEY

Faith is the key to things not seen, faith is the key to every man's dream, faith is the key that unlocks from within.

Faith is your belief lived over and over again.

Faith is love, peace, and joy.

Faith is the fulfillment of every man's void.

So when in your life you go through trials and tribulations, remember one thing you must be patient.

Now use the key of faith to unlock the door, than through this life you shall truly soar.

You've unlocked the door to see what is on the other side, you have found Jesus now in him abide.

His spirit will always see you through, remember the key is inside of you.

Jesus is the master key to God the Father eternally.

Frank V. Moran
1-19-2002

THE EXTREME

Young people you take life to the extreme, at least that's how it seems, your ancestors died that you might have dreams.
Young people you take life to the extreme, two hundred dollar tennis shoes, pants hanging down thinking your cool.
Every time I turn on the news another young person charge with abuse, yes pushing dope, yes wild and loose.
Young people you take life to the extreme, I hate to say it but that's how it seems.
Now if you truly want to take life to the extreme, and I really mean being clean.
Make the extreme sacrifice, if you just have to just have to give up your life. You see sacrifice is rooted and bound together, by the God who created us to live forever.

Frank V. Moran
1-19-2002

I AM

I am that man, that boy, that girl, I am the womb of the mothers
that fill this world.
I am that tree that gives you shelter.
I am that homeless person you didn't feed.
I am the lamb that died on Calvary.
I am the little bird that fly's here and there.
I died for people everywhere, even those across the seas.
All I ask is that you believe in me.
I am love, joy and peace.
My love is kind and my raft is sure, when you know me theirs nothing
you can't endure.
I am God.

Frank V. Moran
1-19-2002

Dark Cold is the Night

Dark cold is the night of the run away slave.

I've got to leave this plantation before I am in my grave.

It's about time for me to take flight.

Dark cold is the night, as I run I hear the crack of the whip, no food or clothing for this long cold trip.

Dark cold is the night of the run away slave.

No time to stop!

I hear the howl of the dogs, I'll just float across the river on this here old log.

I believe they is coming I hear the sound of the dogs.

I know if they catch me, they will strip my back.

So hears a message for you brother on that modern day crack.

Dark cold is the night of the run away slave.

Maybe their a life I can truly save before master puts me in my grave.

In my mind I feel the tightening of the rope.

In my dreams I see that modern day dope.

They have sold my wife and children too, nothing else but to run yes that what I'll do.

Dark cold is the night.

Gonna go home and be with my Lord where I'll be in the arms of God.

Dark cold is the night.

Frank V. Moran
1-19-2002

A Glimmer of Hope

There's yet still a glimmer of hope, as we strive to achieve and learn
to cope.
Yes theirs still a glimmer of hope, as we teach our children and yes
they take notes.
There's yet still a glimmer of hope if we teach morals and values and
not selling dope.
Now before you take a career in dealing dope; remember there is
yet still a glimmer of hope.
Back in time they used a rope, its 2001 now they are using dope.
So teach your children it doesn't matter their color in God's eyesight
were all sisters and brothers.
So before you give up on life, there's a glimmer of hope.
He will brighten your life, my Lord and Savior Jesus Christ.

Frank V. Moran
1-19-2002

So You Thought You Killed This Race

So you thought you killed this race
Different time same place right here in this United States.
You yet have to look in the face, of another black man that is willing
to take a stand.
Maybe you would have killed this race, had it not been for God's
amazing grace.
So you thought you killed this race.
I am not being prejudice but I want this poem to register.
In all do fairness I'm trying to raise awareness.
There is no superior race only God's amazing grace
We must all face in another place, the only one God's begotten son.
So you thought you killed this race.
God always has a ram in the bush, who's willing to push the walls of
oppression down.
Their was Rosa Parks that brought us out of the dark.
It's time to be complete and not give up our seats.
We must dream, the dream of Dr. Martin Luther King, we must be
complex as Malcolm X.
This poem is not a mystery, it's all about our history.
You see this race has found its place in God's amazing grace.

Frank V. Moran
1-19-2002

Young People

Young people get a grip, selling drugs and killing thinking you are hip.
Young people take this tip; it's time for you to get a grip.
Young bodies lying in the morgue, young brothers and sisters calling one another dog.
Young people violence is not the solution feeding your mind all that rap pollution.
Now young people you have been told get your life together don't lose your soul.
I too had to get a grip, doing drugs thinking I was hip.
Now God has control of my life, but it came at a price.
Grip the hand of Jesus, the one who gives eternal life for he is the one who paid the price.

Frank V. Moran
1-19-2002

Two Rocks

This is a poem about two rocks.
One is sold on most every block.
This rock will cause pain, misery and strife and when its finished with you it will take your very life.
I guest by now you know this rock's name.
I believe they call it crack cocaine.

Rock number two is steadfast and sure, when you know this rock theirs nothing you can't endure.
I am talking about the rock of our salvation, he can bring you out of any situation.
So when you're tempted by rock number one, just fall on your knees and call on the one.
I am talking about God's only begotten son.
So now you know rock number two, his name is Jesus and he is there for you.

Frank V. Moran
1-19-2002

You Can't Give A Life Back

You can't give a life back, all because you wanted to sell crack.
Now this poem is about to unfold, you've just shot down a two year old.
So now you realize this little girl is paralyzed.
You can't give a life back, and that's a fact.
Most of us don't think we have to worry, young brothers killing over
dope territory.
Can't you see you can't give a life back, just open your eyes and look
at the facts?
Today or tomorrow you'll make your last sale maybe you'll be killed
or wind up in jail.
You can't give a life back.

Frank V. Moran
1-19-2002

THE TRUTH ABOUT DRUGS

THE TRUTH ABOUT DRUGS, IT'S A MORTAL SIN, IT'S A SAD SITUATION
YOU JUST CAN'T WIN.
THE DRUGS YOU DO, YES, YOU MADE THE CHOICE.
BUT NOW IT'S TIME THAT I RAISE MY VOICE.
DRUGS WILL MAKE YOU LIE, CHEAT, AND STEAL.
I WAS A DRUG ADDICT SO I KNOW HOW IT FEELS TO GIVE UP ON
LIFE FOR A FIVE OR TEN DOLLAR HIT, NOW YOU KNOW IT'S A SIN SO
WHY DON'T YOU QUIT.

THE TRUTH ABOUT DRUGS, JUST TO NAME A FEW MARIJUANA,
HEROIN, OH, CRACK-COCAINE TOO, ALSO THE COCAINE YOU SNIFF
UP YOUR NOSE, ONCE YOU'VE DONE THESE DRUGS YOU HAVE LOST
CONTROL.
DRUGS ARE KILLING THE YOUNG AND THE OLD.

THE TRUTH ABOUT DRUGS, HOW IT'S AFFECTING YOU LADIES,
CAN'T YOU SEE YOU'RE HAVING CRACK BABIES. DRUGS WILL EVEN
MAKE YOU SELL YOUR BODIES, AND NOW YOU HAVE AIDS AND
DON'T KNOW HOW YOU GOT.

THE TRUTH ABOUT DRUGS, NOW YOU KNOW IT'S NOT RIGHT,
IT'S TIME FOR ALL TO CLEAN UP YOUR LIFE.
SO IF YOU WANT TO GET OFF DRUGS, TAKE MY ADVICE,
SEEK YE THE ONE, WHO PAID THE ULTIMATE PRICE, I AM TALKING
ABOUT MY LORD AND SAVOIR JESUS CHRIST.

THAT'S HOW I BECAME CLEAN, I LET JESUS IN, AND THAT'S HOW I BECAME CLEAN OF MY SINS.
AT FIRST, IT MAY SEEM A LITTLE HARD, BUT YOU CAN DO IT WITH THE LOVE GOD.

THE TRUTH ABOUT DRUGS, IT TOOK AWAY EIGHT YEARS OF MY LIFE, BUT NOW I HAVE JESUS CHRIST.

I WROTE THIS POEM IT'S LIKE A SHORT STORY, IT TELLS OF GOD'S LOVE AND GLORY.

THIS POEM IS ALSO FOR DRUG DEALERS, STOP SELLING THOSE DRUGS AND BECOME SPIRITUAL HEALERS.
OH, YES, I'VE SOLD DRUGS, TOO AND THAT'S WHY I AM TRYING TO APPEAL TO YOU.
KILLING YOUR BROTHERS AND SISTERS FOR FANCY CLOTHES AND NEW CAR, EVEN SOME OF YOU WHO SHOULD BE UPHOLDING THE LAW.

THE TRUTH ABOUT DRUGS, IT'S A MORTAL SIN, BUT GOD IS WAITING TO TAKE YOU IN.
JUST REMEMBER ONE THING IT'S THE PLAIN TRUTH.
I ONCE WAS A DRUG ADDICT TOO.

FRANK V. MORAN
1999

EXPRESSIONS OF LIFE

FRANK V. MORAN

DEDICATION

This book of God given poetry is to up lift and educate people all across this globe of the many problems and occurrences, that cut us off from the love of God. Even though God said he would never leave or forsake us, we as his children can anger him. To those of you with different beliefs, whom are from different countries, may God bless you, your people, and most of all your children. These expressions of life, I have seen through the eyes of God. I shall always pray for peace throughout the world.

Frank V. Moran
2003

TABLE OF CONTENTS

Spirits *23*

From the Heights or Heaven *24*

Severed Ties *25*

I Ain't But Five *26*

I Need You Lord *27*

Shame or Blame *28*

No Longer, World Hunger *29*

Do You Know What It Takes? *30*

War Cries *31*

Prayer *32*

The Essence of Blackness *33*

Let Us *34*

God's Gonna Wipe All *35*

Spirit's

As I sleep I see the spirit's of the living and the dead.
Sometimes as I sleep, what I see makes me weep.

Brothers and sisters coming over on ships, some already dead
some with broken hips. I see the backs of the blacks stripped
by the whip, I see the crimson stain given by the master's hand.

Blood flowing like a river just the thought of it makes me shiver.
As I sleep I feel the weight of the chains. As I sleep I ask God
to take away the pain. But he says write on son this must never
happen again.

Brothers and sisters use your gifts, don't let your spirit be stripped.
Pass it on, to another tell the story to a brother. Tell them the truth
and tell them the facts. I see the spirit's of the living and the dead.
Yes God is hurting, I feel his pain but he keep on giving over and
over again. So open your hearts and make a decision before we
wind-up in a collision. God's not pleased with this division. I see the
spirit's of the living and the dead.

Frank V. Moran
2003

From the Heights of Heaven

From the height of heaven God extended the palm of his hand, stuck it deep down in the mother land.

This soil is dark and rich, I know it will stand, I'll use it to create a man.

As God molded and shaped him, and gave him arms, in a matter of seconds a man was born.

God talked to man told him how to live now the breath of life I shall truly give.

Now life in the garden was truly serene, but God saw that man needed a queen. So God touched the man, and he began to dream.

From the side of man he created a queen. They lived together oh so serene. God said remember to love, I gave you that power, and if you do this many gifts I will always shower. From the height of heaven God extended the palm of his hand.

Frank V. Moran
2003

Severed Ties

Man's roots are tied together, even if some people say never.

You see when we as people live a lie we bring on severed ties. We severed the ties between man and God and that what makes life really hard.

Let me give you a sample, here an example. Megdar Evers bent the rules he just wanted to attend college, to gain himself some wisdom and knowledge. You see knowledge comes from all mighty God and the spirit of his son, our Savior and Lord.

Everytime one of God chosen ones dies, we find ourselves living a lie, and that's truly what brings on severed ties. It's time for us to open our eyes and don't cut the cord to almighty God, don't sever the ties.

Frank V. Moran
2003

I Ain't but Five

I ain't but five but I feel sick, today. My father tells me to kneel and pray.

He tells me to pray in whatever I do, I am young but I need God to.

At the age of five I realize, I needed to be baptized.

At this age I don't know all about God, but I know I love the Lord, got to go now I still feel sick, got to say me a prayer real quick. Sometimes my dad he gets sick, but I see him pray real real quick.

I ain't but five.

Frank V. Moran
2003

I Need You Lord

I need you Lord, so I can prevail, I am like a ship that has let down
its sail. I am troubled by all these females.

I do believe it's only the lust of the flesh. Here comes another I dare
not touch.

I love my wife I dare not sin, here comes a female with a grin.
God you gave me love you gave me power that's why we talk
every second, every minute, every hour.

Here comes another around the bend, hoist my sail blow your
wind. Protect me from this storm of life, that I might not pay the
ultimate price. I need you Lord.

Frank V. Moran
2003

Shame or Blame

Young girl walking in shame now I wonder, whose the blame. All because she wouldn't abstain. Now don't leave out the young man, I do believe he too shares the blame.

Now she walks the streets, her young head hung down, the young man who played his part is no where around.

Only if she had stayed in her text and not experience sex. The young man told her to have an abortion. Instead of standing up giving his portion. Young girl, you need not be stressed, God has put you through a test, you don't have to be ashamed or blamed, just abstain. God would rather here a baby cry than to know that one just died.

Frank V. Moran
2003

No Longer, World Hunger

As I open the cabinet, I have more than I need but I can't help but think about the children over seas. I see world hunger, even in this nation, we must do something about this situation. I see children, nothing but skin and bones some will die all along. God has blessed this world too much than to let his children turn to dust. The world is full of famine and disease, you must truly know God is not pleased. This situation we must address, we must plant the seeds and God will do the rest. We must stretch our arms far and wide just like the crimson tide, the one who stretches his arms and died.

No longer, world hunger.

Frank V. Moran
2003

Do You Know What It Takes?

Do you know what it takes to be a mother or father? Taking care or your sons and daughters. Stand strong, be firm, yet be patient.

Hold on to this new generation, because they are like tender vegetation.

We mothers and fathers are like soil from the ground, so the lives of our children we must surround.

We are the nutrients that shape their lives the most important nutrient is Jesus Christ.

Take them to church and send them to school, let them know that life has rules.

So when you as their mother's and father's are in doubt, call on God he will bring you out. Do you know what it takes?

Frank V. Moran
2003

In the back of my mind, I hear the cry of war. I know some country has been torn apart.

I hear the bombs as they fall from the sky, I hear the voices of the children that died, also the sound of mother's that cry.

Can't you hear the whistle of another in-coming missile?

As the bombs hit, I see broken bones, as another one hits I see broken homes. Why we as people don't use our head? Why must our streets run red?

God has blessed us near and far, their should be no need for war.

Let every nation share love, joy, and peace, it's time for war to cease. I know wars are fought over something, but most are fought over nothing. So let us think before we push a button. If we cry, let it be tears of joy, let us think before the troops are deployed. In the back of my mind I hear the cry of war.

Frank V. Moran
2003

Prayer

When you kneel down to pray, just to let all mighty God have is way. When you're burdened down by life's trials and tribulations, remember God has already got a hold on your entire situation.

Give him your burdens, give him your pain, and through his love he will pick you up, over and over again.

When you kneel down to pray, don't think to hard of what to say, just use your voice and talk to God, and don't leave out Jesus our Lord.

You see God has already answered your prayer, he holds the key he's everywhere.

When you kneel down to pray, just add an ounce of faith, and God has already changed your state.

When you kneel down to pray.

Frank V. Moran
2003

The Essence of Blackness

The essence of blackness is not, just a color, it's striving, achieving, and loving your brother.

The essence of blackness is calling your elders Mr. or simply respecting your black sisters.

The essence of blackness must be bold, if the blackness inside you is to unfold.

So in these words you didn't understand, I believe you had better read it again.

The essence of blackness so, in this life, when you feel troubled, read, these words it tells all about the black struggle.

Sometimes the essence will cause you pain, don't worry about that, just read it again.

The essence of blackness.

Frank V. Moran
2004

Let Us

Let us bathe in the debts of his dying love, let us follow in the footsteps of his wisdom, that came from above, let us greet the morning and everyday, with knowledge from on high that paved the way. Let us remember it's not all about a color, but how we treat our sisters and brothers. Let us remember he did the work of the Lord, he stood on the words of almighty God.

Let us remember Dr. Martin Luther King, and never let us forget to dream the dream.

In honor of Dr. Martin Luther King, Jr.

May the truth of his life and the words he spoke lift you to a new plateau in life.

Frank V. Moran
2004

God's Gonna Wipe All

God's gonna wipe all.
God's gonna wipe all.
God's gonna wipe all your tears away.

God told Noah to build the ark it rained so hard and then it got dark.

The children of Israel, were truly slaves, but God told Moses to go and save.

God's gonna wipe all.
God's gonna wipe all.
God's gonna wipe all your tears away.

Shadrack, Meshack and Abednego, was tried in the fire with the Holy Ghost.

They nailed my Jesus to a cross, he suffered, bled and died for all the lost.

God's gonna wipe all.
God's gonna wipe all.
God's gonna wipe all your tears away.

Got to pick that cotton, got to work those fields, got to pick that cotton just to get a meal.

You young people, you better take note, we're the black people that came over on boats.

God's gonna wipe all.
God's gonna wipe all.
God's gonna wipe all your tears away.

Broken backs and broken hips, can't you hear the crack of the whip.

You need to get down, on your knees, and the word of God you shall truly receive.

God's gonna wipe all.
God's gonna wipe all.
God's gonna wipe all your tears away.

A cold black man came on the scene why did they kill, Martin Luther King?

This brother wasn't the enemy, but they killed John F. Kennedy.

Children you might have to go to your grave, but at least it's better than being a slave.

God's gonna wipe all.
God's gonna wipe all.
God's gonna wipe all your tears away.

Now let me take you back in time, let me share a vision of mine.

The war was bloody without a doubt, the war was waged yes the north against the south.

Now teach this message to your kids, so don't make the same mistakes we did.

God's gonna wipe all.
God's gonna wipe all.
God's gonna wipe all your tears away.

Frank V. Moran
2004
13-3